THE RIGHTEOUS SHALL FLOURISH LIKE THE PALM TREE PSALM 92:12

All Believers in Jesus Christ Must Bear Their Own Fruit

Jeremiah T. Kugmeh

Published in the United States of America

ISBN 978-1-960684-21-9 (SC)
ISBN 978-1-960684-19-6 (HC)
ISBN 978-1-960684-20-2 (Ebook)

Jeremiah Kugmeh Publication
205 dudley pl.
new castle, de 19720
www.stellarliterary.com

Order Information and Rights Permission:

Quantity sales. Special discounts might be available on quantity purchases by corporations, associations, and others. For details, contact the publisher at the address above.

For Book Rights Adaptation and other Rights Permission.
Call us at toll-free 1-888-945-8513 or send us an email at admin@stellarliterary.com.

AUTHOR: JEREMIAH T. KUGMEH

Jeremiah T. Kugmeh: BSC Economics: Monrovia, Liberia
MSC Human Services and Organizational leadership.
Springfield college, Massachusetts, USA

AUTHOR'S NOTE

To some a palm tree is thought of as a tree of decoration, or a tree embedded in our secular consciousness. Conversely, the Bible refers to it as a tree of righteousness and is symbolic of fruit-bearing Christians. Therefore, to all *believers* and fruit bearing Christians who are privileged to read this book, beware that you are not exempted from facing challenges, temptations, and obstacles at various times and places. Understanding that God's will for you is to flourish and succeed in every area of life, including relationships, career aspirations, addictions and recovery, ill-health and sound mind, as well as spiritual life and discipleship. The Lord has not set you up for failure instead he deposited within you a seed of greatness which elevates your purpose over your struggle. Therefore, all pastors, evangelists, teachers of the gospel and church workers are welcome to use this book as reference and Bible study guide.

Contents

Dedication.. vi

Introduction.. vii

Background.. viii

Forward... ix

Chapter 1 The Usefulness of Palm Trees in West Africa.....................1

Chapter 2 The Righteous Shall Flourish Like the Palm Tree 10

Chapter 3 Palm Trees Have A Covenant Relationship with the Soil...........14

Chapter 4 Fruit Bearing Christians Must Flourish............................17

Chapter 5 Palm Trees Have the Ability to Thrive............................21

Chapter 6 Palm Tree Can Not Be Grafted 26

Chapter 7 Life of a Palm Tree is On The Inside 32

Chapter 8 Palm Trees have the Ability to Bend and not Break 34

Chapter 9 Palm Trees Cannot be Used as Wood..................................36

Chapter 10 Palm Trees Have The Ability to Share External Ills 39

Chapter 11 Palm Trees Have the Ability to Withstand Shame,
          Abuse, and Disgrace...42

Chapter 12 A Palm Tree is Evergreen...45

Chapter 13 Palm Trees Can Bind Together and Provide
          A Place of Refuge..47

Chapter 14 The Older the Palm Tree, the Sweeter the Fruit................49

DEDICATION

This book is delightfully dedicated to Pastors Morgan and his wife Jennifer Ikonne of Rebuilders Apostolic Ministries for their unflinching commitment to the preaching, teaching and mentoring of a diverse congregation of believers. I recalled when Satan deceitfully attacked my soul with news of prostate cancer in 2017. My blood pressure flared up through the roof. I was at the mercy of the medical doctors while pharmaceutical industries were celebrating the prospect of another procedural patient and profit-making entity. Thankfully, the Lord intervened on my behalf when the Lord spoke through Pastor Morgan Ikonne. He suggested that I should not consider surgery as a treatment option because he has heard my cry for help. I took heed to his Divine Wisdom and now I thank God for healing me. My gratitude also goes to all members of the Rebuilders Apostolic Ministries for their prayers. I proudly dedicate the book to my wife Pauline for her spiritual counsel and I pay particular homage to the project committee members headed by Sister Delphine Ndifor and Brother Divine Abanke for their hard work, vision and unfailing commitment to rally the congregation to raise funds to relocate the increasing congregation. To all department heads, I say thanks for the work you do for Rebuilders Apostolic Ministries. Finally, to my friend Michael Harris who edited the manuscript prior to submission to the publishing company. Furthermore, my grandchildren; MaRhoda and Lucia Seh, should know Grandpa says, "I love you dearly". As you embark on the journey to living a flourishing life, let the sky be the limit.

INTRODUCTION

I was fortunate to have an opportunity to teach a Bible Study class at Rebuilders Apostolic Ministries in Bear, DE, US. My curriculum emphasized the text in Psalm 92:12. After I reviewed this biblical passage, a couple of things surprised me. First, I was amazed to learn that there is an indisputable spiritual connection between a fruit bearing Christian and a palm tree. In addition, there were no references to affluent personalities the like Warren Buffet and Bill Gates. Instead, the Bible told us how all Christians will flourish like a palm tree. I learned from the Holy Scripture that as a true believer and follower of Jesus Christ, the Lord has promised all the fruit-bearing Christians the gift of righteousness and to flourish like a palm tree.

In order to assess the position of all Christians relative to this reading, I decided to research the topic. My objective was to get a better understanding about the nature, structure, and characteristics of a palm tree as it relates to righteousness and success.

I became terrified when I was called upon to fulfill my obligation to offer instruction to my fellow church members. I had not taught a Bible lesson in 15 years which made me very apprehensive of my ability to perform this lecture. I prayed and the Lord reminded me that He has not given us the spirit of fear. Instead, we are filled with courage, love, and a sound mind.

Although Pastor Jennifer Ikonne didn't teach, she was prayerfully monitoring and proctoring all the weekly teachings. During my teaching moment, I learned I had to invite the Holy Spirit to help me in my preparation to expound on the topic I desired to teach. The Lord miraculously enlightened my understanding of Psalm 92:12, "The righteous shall flourish like the palm tree and grow like the cedar in Lebanon." I know palm trees very well but my knowledge of cedar is limited. Therefore, speaking from my life experience with palm trees, the Lord wanted me to convey a message and secret of living a fruitful life as a believer. Please join me as we study the relationships between a palm tree and fruit bearing Christians.

BACKGROUND

Rev. Morgan Ikonne, the Senior Pastor of the church had scheduled three of the members currently serving on the leadership board to teach weekly Bible Studies while he was on his biblical mission in Africa. Among those chosen to teach Bible study was Brother James Johnson, the church administrator and treasurer. He taught on the topic "Stewardship" for one hour thirty minutes. I was the second lecturer and fittingly as the author of this book, the topic I discussed was, "Fruitfulness in Christians living". Thereafter, Associate Pastor Marco Eyong, the man with a unique and spirited gift of prayer was scheduled to teach on the "Fruit of the Holy Spirit". Pastor Jennifer Ikonne offered her insight, prayer, and direction to the aforementioned speakers.

Again, my main text was taken from Psalm 92:12 and after reading it I learned a couple of things which shocked me to the core of my heart. First, I was amazed to learn that there is an indisputable spiritual connection between a fruit bearing Christian and a palm tree. Secondly, I was astonished to learn that to bear more fruits as Christians we must follow the example of a palm tree. Thirdly, the natural structure of a palm is similar to that of a human being. Lastly, the word of God has assured the gift of righteousness and flourishing life to all fruit bearing Christians. In order to assess my position as a Christian and that of others who are found to be in the household of God, I became compelled to research the topic to get a better understanding about the nature, structure, and characteristics of a palm tree as it relates to righteousness and successful living in the world and beyond. I have known and used palm products for decades but cedar, I have not seen. Fellow Christians, please join me as we study the relationships between a palm tree and fruit bearing Christians, which figuratively portrays the tree as the son of the living God. This book is written in two distinctive phases regarding the palm tree: Firstly, it draws on the usefulness of a palm tree and its products in most developing societies. I also investigate the relationship between a palm tree and living a flourishing life as Christians. Good Luck and blessings to my fellow man.

FORWARD

The profound thing about reading a book for us is not the style of writing which the author employs, nor the title that the author chooses. It is the "Simplicity" by which the author elucidates his concept in such a way that the simplest minded among us could read and understand. The brilliant minds among us can stay engaged and analytical upon deciphering these insightful pages of his literary commentary. Mr. Jeremiah Kugmeh has held such swaged on us as we read this book. His conceptualization of the "Palm Tree" is both profound and consistent with Biblical Truth. Biblical revelation is both practical and relevant and, in this book, "The Palm Tree" Mr. Jeremiah Kugmeh has elucidated such practical application and practical relevance of The Palm Tree and its connectivity to successful Christian living. In this book, the author engages the reader with pragmatic biblical revelation on how "The Palm Tree" relates to us as Believers. The palm branch is a symbol of victory, triumph, peace, and eternal life. A palm branch was awarded to victorious athletes in ancient Greece. Furthermore, a palm frond or the tree itself is one of the most common attributes of Victory personified in ancient Rome.

This book is a necessary read by all believers who desire to grow and be successful in their Christian walk. As Pastors, we have had the privilege of knowing the author of this book as a Leader in our Local Church. We know the in-depth value he places on the Word of God and its practical relevance to Life here on Earth. It is our belief that you will become greatly blessed as you read this book.

Pastor Morgan & Jennifer Ikonne

Senior Pastors

Rebuilders Apostolic Ministries Inc

Bear Delaware USA

Chapter 1

THE USEFULNESS OF
PALM TREES IN WEST AFRICA

The structure of a palm tree is much like the body of a human being. For instance, when the head of a palm tree is cut off the palm tree will die, whereas other trees can survive decapitation. The heart or life of a palm tree lies within its external body. Analogously, the soul of a human being is internal. Therefore, it is not a surprise why the word of God says the Lord is calling on all believers and fruit-bearing Christians to be like the palm tree if they wish to flourish spiritually. In this chapter we will carefully examine the usefulness of a palm to humanity. Before going forward with an examination of the connection between the characteristics of palm trees and Christendom and religiosity let us look at the practical usefulness of the palm tree to mankind. It is noteworthy to specify that the palm tree is significant in the economic, social, political, and religious life of Liberia which is my country of origin.

A. Economic Usefulness of a Palm tree in Liberia

The following are the usages of a palm tree for the various ethnic groups within Liberia. With a population of approximately four million people, the rural sector relies heavily on the products extracted from palm trees. The tree is very important for various economic reasons relevant to the tribal people of which 75% of whom have no access to refined and manufacturing products that are imported from more developed industrial societies. For instance, Zinc is hardly affordable. Therefore, the branches of palm trees are used in rural Liberia to roof huts often referred to as houses. Prior to the importation of western types of cabbage, tribal people ate palm cabbage. This vegetation serves as the fruit production center of all palm trees. The widespread consumption of palm cabbage by tribal people has led to mass extinction of this sapling in other parts of the country. Palm cabbage is often the only nutritional alternative to alleviate hunger in many regions in the countryside.

Tribal people are able to produce wine from palm cabbage for income generation and for home consumption. Native Liberians call it palm wine. It sells very fast at the local market because it has multiple addictive properties. A villager can sell a gallon of wine and get a cake of soap, a pair of slippers, two cups of rice, a piece of fresh meat, or fish in return. This type of exchange is referred to as the barter system meaning there is no exchange of money but has its own demand and supply phenomenon.

Palm flakes generate cooking oil. The thickness of the palm flakes determines the quantity of cooking oil that can be produced from one palm bunch. The juice that is extracted from the fruit is used to formulate the product which is often referred to as palm butter. Palm butter is a useful and exact substitute of the peanut butter that is produced in the west and sold to African nations at an exorbitant price cost. Africans have little or no access to the nutritional attributes of western butter products and have little alternatives to the limited nutritional values in palm butter. The extraction process for various palm butter derivatives is very tedious and time consuming. The palm tree fruits are placed into a waiting clay iron pot and set over the fire. It is left there to boil for about two hours before it gets softer. Several of the fruits are placed or empty into a mortar and pounded until the shelves come off and completely separated from the kernels. The juice collected from the palm kernels is used for making bathing soap, laundry soap, cream or medication. When the palm is mixed with baking soda, we get the laundry soap. After the shelves and kernels are separated and the juice is carefully extracted from the palm nuts, the kernels and hard covering of the nuts are placed in a remote area to dry. The dried kernels are cracked open with a piece of iron to retrieve edible nuts out. The nuts usually come out smashed or rounded and then nuts are parched over a fire in an iron pot to get the second level of another type of cooking oil; usually it turns out black or white. The juice that comes from inside the nuts can be used to pour over cooked rice for consumption or mixed with perfume to be used as an after-bath cosmetic for cream. Many bunches grow on the Palm tree in West Africa and on each bunch, there are hundreds of fruits. Inside every fruit is a kernel that is shelled with a very hard protective covering that is very difficult to crack. On the outer part of the kernel there exist flakes which determine if the fruit is ripe for harvesting or not.

The peelings from the palm branches are used for mats to sleep on or and the dried branches of the palm tree are attached together to make doors and windows for our huts/houses. The raw or dried branches of palm trees are used to make water traps or fences around gardens and farms to deter the invasion of rodents and other undesirable animals. Palm leaves are also worn as clothing during special traditional ceremonies.

B. Medical Benefits of Palm Trees

The cream produced from the aforementioned juice can treat skin rashes, ringworm and sores as a substitute to scarcely available western medication. Oil extracted from the dried kernel can be used to treat fever and headaches. Rubbing a blend of the oil and cinnamon oil or methylation over your temples and back will help you sweat out many illnesses. It can also be used for deworming. When the oil comes from ripe flesh fruits it destroys hookworm and ringworm. Adults and children can consume one teaspoon in the morning and evening. It is also popular among people growing their natural hair as it is good for dandruff. Your hair will also thank you for the treatment. The oil is traditionally used to protect the body against various forms of cancer and is a good laxative for improving digestion and bowel function. This is not only good in your food, but it can also be used to treat certain eye infections by using it to rinse the infected area. Got a sore throat? It is recommended to drink two tablespoons of oil milk three times a day. Be careful! Don't overdo it as it might upset your tummy. If you are suffering from constipation, drinking half a glass of palm kernel oil will do the trick. The oil is good for relieving muscular pain. Collect some leaves from the heart of the tree, boil them and drink the solution. Another way to cure the muscle aches is to bathe in the mixture.

The liquid obtained from palm kernel oil is said to be a wondrous treatment for people suffering from urinary tract infections and other urinary related problems. It is an energizing drink and is said to be good for kidney and bladder related diseases as well. They have extremely high electrolyte content; the oil contains potassium and is a natural source of Vitamin C. It has a calming effect on stomach aches. The roots can be used to treat gall bladder and as well as kidney related diseases by boiling four or five well-washed roots in some lightly salted water and drinking upon cooling. For those suffering from eczema, wash the area with the mixture of roots. For Fibrosis, boil three to five finger-long pieces of roots and drink it for approximately three days. It helps melt clotted blood. The roots can also be used to treat heartburn.

In Liberia, the Gio and Mano tribes used red palm oil in treatments of mysterious diseases. To awaken a patient from a coma, red palm oil was mixed with a burned knot of certain parasites. It is rubbed on the patient's cheeks toward the mouth in order to make him talk. Another magical medicine was prepared from any branch broken off by wind but lodged before it reached the ground when mixed with some burned plants. The paste is put into a little horn tied to a cut off cow's tail. The traditional healer asked the sick man a question while brushing his face with the tail. If there was no answer, it is believed that the patient would die. If the patient answers, the healer puts some of this medicine with his left third finger, and rubs it over the patient's heart while saying specific prayers. The broken but not fallen branch perhaps symbolizes hope for the patient to wake up. The palm oil can be used to blend various added ingredients. It was previously used to heal fractures in Liberia. A few branches from various shrubs and trees were gathered, together with any broken twig which was healed but growing in a twisted position. The charred wood was mixed with red palm oil, and the ointment was then applied to the fracture. The twisted branch probably symbolized the twisted limb.

Another example of non traditional medicinal practices that included the palm tree among the Mano was utilization of it as a cure for acute hepatitis. Shelf fungi shaped like a liver were mixed with oil and rubbed over the liver. To remedy heart palpitations, the Mano mixed red palm oil in an artful manner. The mixture was then put in an iron spoon with four pebbles that had been heated in a fire. There would be three pebbles used if the patient was a female. Notably, the stone represented longevity and strength. The red color of palm oil as well as the red sap symbolized the color of the treated heart.

Gender specific symbolic medicines were also used in Liberia for rheumatism with the leaves and bark of living plants and red palm oil, which represented the active male elements. The charred plants and "burned" oil represented the soothing, magical, more preventive female elements. Male and female medicines were mixed in order to form an even more powerful Mano medicine, and possibly to achieve an ideal balance between active and controlled features of each specific person and unique situations.

Women in Liberia used to protect themselves from getting sick with constant consumption of red palm oil. The medicine was tied to the woman's waist and licked from the finger whenever she felt dizzy or afraid. Although in many ritual medicines palm oils served merely as a rubbing agent. In Liberia, palm kernel oil was applied with owl's feathers on wounds resulting from scarring inflicted during the Poro initiation rites. In Cameroon, fresh palm kernel seeds were mashed and mixed with other plants to treat mental fatigue. The residues of medicine were put under the pillow, and only if the patient dreamed of a young girl with erect breasts was there hope for cure. The palm kernel seeds were also used as sacred objects in rituals involved in oracles, which helped to discover the cause of disease or other calamities.

In Zambia splints made of palm mats were tied around broken limbs with bark strips, and medicine was applied on the skin under the mats. Simultaneously, the legs of a chicken were broken and treated with the same medication. The belief is that when the chicken starts to walk again, so will the patient.

Palm leaves were used as protective barriers. A string made of fibers extracted from the palm leaf was suspended on poles in front of the hut as a warning sign for pregnant women. If a pregnant woman entered a hut where there was a baby, its skull would part into pieces. Palm fronds are still used in Benin as sacrifices used to heal a dying person by exchanging the life of an animal for that of the person. Ritual palm fronds mark the sacred spot. Palm frond was also worn around the throat, for protection from witchcraft, or from being killed during war. In Benin, palm fronds are also carried by people involved in punishment of social deviants, and those suspected of witchcraft. During the recent 'witch parades' organized to punish and march the accused Beninese women to prison; the suspected witches were bedecked in wreaths of palm fronds. Perhaps palms bring justice because they are associated with understanding, peace, and harmony, or with indwelling tree spirits themselves. In South Africa a thief was punished by confrontation with palm leaves. Through a form of supernatural judgment, the offender is turned into snakes.

In Nigeria, to recover from smallpox, palm wine was drunk and rubbed on the body of the patient. Relatives were advised not to sleep near an infected person, nor visit anyone outside. Roasted groundnuts were not to be eaten during an epidemic, and no drumming could be performed. For successful recovery it was also necessary to make an offering to the tribal god by sprinkling palm wine all over the house to appease the god. Ancestral spirits appreciate these drinks, and palm wine was often used in offerings and fetishes to obtain their favor and help to reduce their anger. Therefore, this reduced the risk of disease or another calamity. To engage a powerful and influential person in a relationship of beneficial exchange and prosperity, palm wine was shared as a valued consumable beverage or lubricant. It is believed to foster good relations and hospitality. In Kenya, the Mijikenda people place coconut shells filled with palm wine on ancestors' graves as an offering.

The Mano of Liberia carried amulets for protection against witchcraft, made from small horns with enclosed palm wine and a charred powdered twig. By licking the medicine from the finger, a person was ensured that if anyone wanted to bewitch him, he would expose their devious exploits, and subsequently be made accountable for their malevolent actions.

Although most medicines were directed toward the cure and prevention of disease, some could also embrace poisons. In Liberia, a poisonous mixture was prepared while calling the name of the victim, put under the thumbnail and then placed in a gourd of palm wine. The victim was offered the lethal drink, always using the left hand.

C. Socio-Political Benefits of Palm Trees

Indigenous tribes of tropical regions have long used palm leaves for their fibrous properties to produce woven and hand-crafted household items. Palm leaflets are typically sewn together to form plaits, which constitute the skeletal structure of baskets, mats, sacks, fans and hats. A useful cord is made by rolling leaf fibers into strands. The cord is helpful for tying bundles of plants and vegetables. Palm leaf cords are also used to create nets for transporting cargo and forage. Fishnets and open hammocks are also created with palm leaf cords, while heavier cords act as climbing ropes that are used to scale trees during palm leaf harvesting. Palm leaf fibers are commonly placed within furniture as mattress or cushion stuffing.

Palm leaves of every species have been used as the roofing and partition material of huts. When constructed correctly, palm leaf roofs are extremely durable and water-resistant while remaining porous enough to allow ventilation from cooking flames and promote proper air circulation. A thick mud layer is used for adhering whole palm leaves to the ceiling beams of hatches. Palm leaflets make excellent partitions and terraces. Young, flexible leaves are selected and cut to overlap on top of huts. A palm leaf roof will last for approximately two years, depending on the leaf species and surrounding climate conditions.

Palm leaves are one of the oldest and cheapest writing materials in existence. They were used extensively throughout some parts of Asia as far back as the year 790. To create writing material, partially-matured palm leaves were dried, cut to size and rubbed with oil. The leaves underwent an extensive boiling and oiling process, in order to reduce acid content and close the leave's

6

pores. In this manner, palm leaves were transformed into resilient and waterproof writing material.

The branches of the palm tree are a symbol of conquest, victory, liberation, freedom from oppression, subjection, humiliation, pain, depression, annihilation, and death. The branches of palm trees are used to show ownership and boundary lines. In the traditional African cultures, the presence of palm branches in an obscure place indicates a warning to travelers and villagers. For instance, the villagers usually set aside a hut where midwives carry pregnant women to give birth. Furthermore, when a woman is in pain, their entire living area is sealed up with palm branches. When the god of the tribe is paying a daily visit, only those who are mature, trained and capable of keeping secrets are allowed to enter his presence. Therefore, to deter undesirables the palm branches are used to seal up the entire worship area. Palm branches are a symbol of conflict resolution between warring parties. The victors carry branches of palm trees on their heads while singing, dancing, and feasting. In addition, the palm branches are used during weddings. When an agreement espouses a daughter to a man special arrangement are customarily reached through or by the payment of a dowry. After the marriage is finally consummated friends and relatives of both parties will burst out through the village carrying palm branches in their hands, on their heads, and around their waist while dancing and singing for three to four days. Palm branches are used for social decorations in the urban and rural areas.

D. Role of Palm Tree in Scriptures Ezekiel Chapter 41:18

The cherubim and the palm trees were closely associated in that both were largely represented, and they were found in close conjunction: "a palm tree was between a cherub and a cherub." Both of them pictured the righteous man in the sanctuary of God, but while the cherub signified the good man at his best bringing himself and all that he had as an offering to God. The palm tree is analogous to the good man being one who had been made into what he was by the services of the sanctuary; one was enlarged and embodied humanity bringing its offering to God, the other was that same humanity gaining its goodness and worth from God and from His house. There is a very good reason why a palm tree should reflect a picture of the righteous man. There is also an excellent reason why the prominence of the palm tree in the prophet's vision should picture the truth that man's goodness is the fair and excellent result of much communion with God. Among the resemblances are detailed below:

7

I. ITS UPRIGHTNESS -Some trees are irregular. They are twisted and tortuous in their growth; some hug the ground before they rise; but eventually the palm rises straight toward heaven, it stands upright among other trees. "Like some tall palm the noiseless fabric grew." The good man is well figured here; he is the man who does not stoop, who does not bend and bow earthward, who stands erect, who moves in one heavenward direction, who is governed constantly by true and abiding principles. He gains these attributes from God, and from His house. There, in this sanctuary, he is sustained in his principles, and is reminded of them while gaining fresh inspiration to illustrate and adorn them.

II. ITS FRUITFULNESS - The palm, as a fruit-bearing tree, bears a fruit which is remarkably nutritious – from the date it blossoms it will sustain life for a long time. Man cannot maintain sustenance without the intake of any other kind of food. This speaks to the spirit of an admirable picture of the righteous man. He bears fruit. He is expected to "bear much fruit," and fruit of many kinds which display excellency of spirit, love, joy, peace, long-suffering, etc. All worthy of a life consistent with blamelessness, practical kindness, an earnest effort to do good, patience, a prayerful endeavor to awaken the slumbering, to elevate the fallen, to comfort the sorrowful, and to encourage the feeble. If he does follow these pursuits it is because of his close affiliation with Jesus Christ his Lord. He must be a branch abiding in the vine. He must maintain a very close spiritual connection with Christ. How else can he do this without these ordinances within his house?

III. ITS BEAUTY - The palm tree lends a great charm to the landscape when seen standing in clusters upon the heights perched against the sky. The evergreen foliage makes each particular tree an object of beauty. The righteous man is he whose character is fair, excellent, and admirable when he is what his Master calls on him to manifest. This actually happens when he seeks the strength and refreshment to be found in communion with God. The more he is observed the more he is admired. The picturesque qualities found in him are "lovely and of good report". He is unselfish, pure, considerate, open-handed, patient, brave, loyal, and loving. His goodness, like the foliage of the palm, does not grow near the ground where it can easily be soiled and lost. Instead, it grows high up where lower entities cannot damage or destroy it.

IV. ITS ELASTICITY - The fiber of the palm is so elastic that even when loaded with considerable weights, it still grows resolutely upwards. There may be a failed attempt to hamper a man's growth. If he "dwells in the house of the Lord," he will rise, notwithstanding all that would otherwise check him, to a noble height of virtue.

V. ITS ULTIMATELY TRIUMPHANT - It does not promise much at the beginning. "It is rough to the touch and enveloped in dry bark, but above it is adorned with fruit... so is the life of the elect, despised below, beautiful above; ... down below straitened by innumerable afflictions, but on high it is expanded into a foliage ... of beautiful greenness" (see 2 Corinthians 4:17; Hebrews 12:11).

Chapter 2

THE RIGHTEOUS SHALL
FLOURISH LIKE THE PALM TREE

Are you a righteous Christian? Are you godly? One can't be simultaneously godly and devilish. It simply doesn't work. Many have tried to be both and they find themselves in a vicious cycle of misery. Are you flourishing like a palm tree? Don't panic, I have good news for you. As long as you are a fruit-bearing Christian, you are flourishing because all your needs are deposited in glory. You don't need a bank card to withdraw your needs from glory. The access card to your bank account in glory is called faith. The Bible says, the just shall live by His faith, not the pastor's faith nor the church's faith. Scriptures state one should strive to be like a palm tree which bears fruits in and out of seasons. This assertion is not an imposition, but rather a reminder about who you are and who you are not. The disclaimer is righteousness cannot be bought or earned through hard labor, regularly attending church, or being born within a Christian bloodline. Righteousness is a gift from God and is only for those who surrender their lives to Christ convicted to do his will and maintain the structure and characteristic of a palm tree. Righteousness speaks to the exact nature of God which is planted in us when we accept Jesus Christ as our lord and savior. Note the words spoken in 1 John 4:17. "Love has been perfected among us in this: that we may have boldness on the Day of Judgment; because as He is, so are we in this world." This verse powerfully references that as sons of God we have the gift of righteousness which qualifies us to live a successful and prosperous life on earth and in eternity. The scripture expresses that we don't have to waste our resources and time acquiring knowledge that is fruitless and has no significance or permanent bearing on our future with Christ. Reflecting on psalm 92:12, let us be reminded that there are three stages of humanity: Six to nine months in the bellies of our mothers, 70 to 90 years to walk the earth and larger world, then after that we must submit to the period of eternity which is either in hell or heaven.

As inspired by the writer of Psalm 92:12, the Scripture clearly says that the secret to acquiring wealth, living a healthy abundant life in this world, and having an eternity in life is to exercise the gift of righteousness. This means fruit-bearing Christians must follow the example of the palm tree. Conversely, humanity has carved its own path to flourishing and successful living outside of God's plan. The end results are not good. When you read Psalm chapter 23, the Bible says, the Lord will lead us to the path of righteousness which he lavishes on every believer as a gift. This is a unique promise that our Father, the almighty God will lead us to the mountains, down the valleys, through the storm, into the deepest depths of the sea, or across the oceans. The Lord says, there is nothing beneath or above the universe that has the capacity to separate us from His love. The Father retorts a guaranteed statement which says He will never leave us nor forsake us. The Lord promises to lead us because the journey to living a flourishing life and being fruitful as a Christian will not be an easy undertaking. Read and see what happened to Job in the Bible. If the Lord through His word specifically references the palm tree, there must be something very special about it. It is worthy to note that when the 30% of the Holy Scriptures discusses at length the ideology of wealth creation it stresses flourishing like a palm tree has a deeper reward than living a wealthy or successful life that we as Christians must make every effort to learn. The Bible says, we shall know them by their fruits.

So what are the indicators of a righteous Christian? Or how do we know a believer who is living a righteous and fruit bearing life? What promises or ordinances must be fulfilled to be considered a Christian who is bearing the gift of righteousness and bearing fruits? This is how Psalm 37: 37 explains it. "Mark the perfect **man**, and behold the upright, for the end of that **man** is peace." The Bible is not telling us about our past or contemporary life or sin but the end of our days on earth. These are the heritage of the qualities of righteousness. They enjoy peace, but there is no peace for the wicked that continue to disobey God's law, or the believer pretending to love, trust, and worship God. This is a complete hypocrisy. The bad tree will bear bad fruits like false prophets. Here is how Jesus describes the righteousness of a fruit bearing Christian in his sermon on the mount, "The righteous person is a person who is poor in spirit, or, he recognizes his or her spiritual poverty and owns that spiritual poverty. What is it to be poor in spirit? Being poor in spirit is one of the attributes of righteousness, God-reliance, self-confidence, submissiveness to God, and self-determination with the sovereign grace of God." Wow, Jesus did not mention the amount of money in the bank or material possessions that are rudiment in the heart of man. The righteous person mourns because he sees and owns his or her spiritual poverty. The righteous person is meek, or gentle, or exercises self-control. The righteous person is famished for righteousness. He has a consuming appetite for righteousness and his greatest desire is to live for God. . The righteous person is devoted to developing and having a pure heart. He does not merely want to look pure in deeds or by wearing a white rob with hanging bracelets on his neck, and reciting scripture while standing on street corners ensuring to pray out loud, and boast how much tithes or offerings are paid in church. He wants to be pure within because God looks on the heart of man. The righteous person is a peacemaker. He is the kind of person who can help those who are alienated to find reconciliation. The righteous person is willing to endure suffering and mistreatment for Jesus Christ. Let us now study how bad fruit bearing individuals try to contradict Jesus's teachings.

The Pharisees' description of a righteous person was the exact opposite of Jesus' description. According to them, the righteous person was a religiously accomplished person. He had no spiritual poverty to own. By virtue of his accomplishments, he knew he was right, he knew he had God's truth. He could say, as the Pharisees did to Jesus, "By what authority do you do these things?" He could say, "We have Moses on our side, and we are descendants of Abraham defining our lineage." He could tell you in detail what was right and what was wrong in any situation. The righteous person according to the Pharisees took pride in their religious achievements. In the parable of the Pharisee and the publican who were praying at the temple is a typical example. The Pharisee in his prayer is another superb example (Luke 18:9–14). "God, I thank you that I am not like other people who do not do your will. I don't swindle, I am not unjust, I don't commit adultery, and I don't take advantage of other people. I fast two times every week. I give God ten percent of everything I receive, no matter how big or small it is. I am proud of what I am not, and I am proud of what I do. I sit on the front row of the church. I am a deacon, usher, Sunday school teacher, and I can recite many Bible verses."

The righteous person was aggressive as he opposed those, he declared to be God's enemies. When the Pharisees followed Jesus searching for mistakes, they saw his disciples stripping raw grain and eating it on a Sabbath. Jesus never taught the Pharisees one thing simply because they knew everything. They attended all the biblical universities in the world. They were political power brokers and indisputable sons of Abraham. They were convinced that they understood the law and Jesus did not. They unequivocally knew they were right and Jesus was wrong. They preached that they had the right interpretation of God's will and Jesus was misrepresenting God's will. The

Pharisees' perception of a righteous person was in fact actually righteous indignation. It was an act of righteousness to trap someone that you declared was a teaching error. It was an act of righteousness to falsely accuse and discredit someone who was doing what you declared to be evil. It was an act of righteousness to destroy a person who was a religious threat to what you professed was right. The righteous person was ceremonially pure. He ate the right things and washed his hands the right way ensuring to practice the commands regarding body purity. The Pharisees' idea of purity existed in how you used your body, not your emotions, not your motivations, and not your inner being. Purity had nothing to do with the mind and the heart. Is it not easy to see how that reasoning could lead to the mock trials and execution of Jesus?

The righteous person was devoted to justice, to condemning the wrong doers, to destroying those who violated the commandments. It was perfectly consistent with the Pharisees' concept of righteousness to bring the woman captured while committing adultery causing Jesus to say, "The Law of Moses says kill her, so what do you say?" This is not the type of righteousness that flourishes like the palm tree but kills the palm tree.

Chapter 3

PALM TREES HAVE A COVENANT RELATIONSHIP WITH THE SOIL

Just as the palm tree has a permanent relationship with soil, the Christians must have a covenant relationship with God our father. By definition, a relationship is mutual understanding of an agreement or consensus between one or more people. Relationships are often an affiliation, connection, association, or bonding that is based and cemented in trust. History has shown that there is no relationship that lasts forever. Some relationships can last for a day, some a year, some five years, some fifty years, and some even beyond a hundred more years. All relationships eventually die naturally. Healthy relationships are about creating and fostering values and building up one another. Before getting into any relationship ask yourself about the motive or purpose. Do you get involved in a relationship because of appearance, achievements, beliefs, cultural affiliation, religious reason, wealth, or just with selfish greed-based objectives. Father Abraham must have learned a hard and valuable lesson from his ancestors when he made his servant take a vow to go back to his father's land to get a wife for his son Isaac. Abraham was aware that all relationships on earth have an end. So, when you get into a relationship, ask yourself, how long will this relationship last? What are my expectations and what are my expectations? The only relationship that has no end and limit is the one Christians have with the Lord.

As believers and followers of Jesus Christ, we have no other option but to have a covenant relationship with the Father just as a palm tree has with the soil. What transpired between Ruth and Naomi is a typical example of a covenant relationship that Christian must have with their Father. Ruth says, "mother Naomi, from the time we have been together fostering the mother-in-law and daughters-in-law relations, I have known you as a woman of excellent spirit, a virtuous woman, a woman who is going somewhere. Please don't entreat me to leave you. For as long as it may take, how hard it may be from now and then, I will never leave you, your people shall be my people, your God shall be my God. Wherever you go I will be by your side." This kind of confession had led Ruth who was a Moabites from the generation of Lot, to initiate the matrimonial relationship with our Lord Jesus Christ. The story about the genesis of the Moabites is lengthy and I will not expound further on the details. However, let's briefly discuss the generation that came into existence when Lot was told by the Lord to leave Sodom and Gomorrah and flee to the Mountains. Instead, Lot chose to run inside a cave with his two daughters where he was induced to have babies by each of them. When famine hit Judah, a condition which is always temporary due to Israel's relentless attitude of disobedience to God, Naomi and her husband chose to flee Israel. Being rock hearted and stubborn they proceeded unto the land of the Moabites to find a sanctuary with food, peace, and security. Some Christians are similar and run from church to church and have no time to bear spiritual fruits. Instead they struggle to enjoy reaping and feasting on the fruits and glory of mankind. When things get a little hard, they move on with this same attitude of unreliability and fruitlessness.

When Judah started to flourish again, Naomi, who had buried her children and her husband in the land of Moab, had decided to return home to Israel. Without doubt, and unlike other mothers-in-law, Naomi was probably a very good mother-in-law. The two widows, or daughters-in-law, decided to follow her to the land of Israel. Later, Mother Naomi had a change of mind and decided to tell them to return and go back to their people. Ruth refused but Oprah decided to return. So, this story speaks of two different types of relationships. Some relationships are temporary, and others are permanent. If the relationship doesn't work, we must learn to close our eyes and kiss the other goodbye. Although this is contrary to God's purpose for man. You may have no clue that a relationship you enter into sometimes was met only for a moment and you are wasting time, resources, and prayers. You force God's hands to enforce your heart desires. When the Lord decides to visit you and takes you to a higher level, the other spousal relationship cannot withstand surging glory and blessings. Therefore, there has to be separation.

The type of relationship that exist between the palm tree and the soil is a covenant. There is nothing on earth that will separate the love and trust between the palm tree and the soil. Due to the trusting relationship, the palm tree reliably stretches its roots more than a mile into the heart of the soil. This is a clear demonstration of how we as Christians who are called to bear fruits and must grow into the Lord. Read and observe how the apostle Paul coins it,

"For I am persuaded, that neither death, nor life, nor angels, nor principalities, nor powers, nor things present, nor things to come, nor height, nor depth, nor any other creature shall be able to separate us from the love of God, which is in Christ Jesus our Lord." The palm tree understands this principle. As a Christian make every effort to be like a palm tree.

Chapter 4

FRUIT BEARING CHRISTIANS MUST FLOURISH

According to Wikipedia dictionary, flourishing is defined as emotional, psychological and social functioning of a person. This type of definition makes matters worse for me or anyone who seeks to get a better understanding of the word. On the contrary, the Bible defines flourishing as having a peace of mind and I think this is far easier to comprehend. Everyone, including all the billionaires in the world needs a peace of mind. You can place a person in a mansion to live, own the most luxurious vehicle in the world, own a resort on one of the pacific islands and still have no peace of mind. He is like a ku-ku-ju-mu-ku (when you are not in something you don't know). A person may have all the acknowledgement, indescribable wealth, speaks in all languages of the world but leaves his heart unguarded. This lifestyle amounts to creating a room for all the cockroaches, snakes, flies, ants, frogs, lizards and other insects to flunk all doors and windows open for others to come inside.

Due to this complicity, humanity tries to generally define flourishing as living a successful life therefore they struggle to find it anywhere, anyway and any time even if it results in loss of lives. Success can be found in America so most people flood into America particularly the United States to find it. Success is in business so most people go into all kinds of businesses whether legal or illegal to find it. Success is in higher education, so most people spend all their time acquiring student loans for higher level of literal education to find it. Success is in natural resources so economically powerful countries and wealthy people explore, dig into the heart of the soil to find it even if it means colonizing and subduing weaker nations. Success is in pastoral work, so they find a way by stirring up trouble to break away from their original churches, ordaining themselves as bishops, evangelists and pastors to find it. Success is at work so they work two or three jobs and so many hours, weeks, months and years to find it. Success is in polygamy, so they marry so many wives or engage in risky promiscuity to find it. Success is in proliferation so they make every effort to have dozens of children to find it. Success is in a grandiose lifestyle so they struggle to live above and beyond their income to find and live it. Success is in getting married in hope of living a happy life so they pick their specials or partners to find it. Success is in career building so they spend all the time, energy and resources acquiring professional skills to find it. Lastly, success is in sports, they abandon early education, associate themselves with sport enthusiasts, align themselves with career sport sponsors, and join teams to play games for pay to find it. Judging the characteristic and relativity of the word, the Biblical definition is highly recommendable. Are your mind and heart at peace in spite of what is happening in the world? at work? in your family? Community and in your life? If your answer is yes, then rise up and shine for the glory of the Lord has risen upon you. If your response is no, then get ready to position the peace of God in your heart which passes all understanding. As a Christian, a true believer and fruit bearing Christians must pray for the peace of God that constantly abides.

The world's interpretation of living a flourishing or successful life is quite different from what the word of God says. For instance, nearly everyone is looking for ways on how to flourish in life, to be successful, to grow and develop economically, to be happy, to live in a five to six-bedroom house that is located on ten acres of land adjacent to the ocean. Their understanding of success is to own and ride the most expensive and modern car in town with tinted glasses, eat whatever they want, travel around the world and frequent 4-star hotels. They wear gold bracelets on their arms, expensive gold chains around their necks, piercing their ears, tongues and navels. Some drive their cars in public playing loud music, wearing eccentric sunshades, expensive wristwatches, and living a grandiose flamboyant life. When the sounds of music are silent, the lights are out, the streets are calmed, restaurants are closed, bars are shut down then they come into what they call home to meet their real selves, the mounting debts, and emotionally conflicted minds generated by truly unfulfilled dreams of self-deception and despair. Secular issues like family abuse, neglect, unheeding health problems, unpaid debts, and disgruntled partners overwhelm their serenity. People travel from country to country, making news of fame, seeking the right selfish opportunities, working very hard for companies, and individuals who are wealthy in hopes that their personal desires will be accomplished from the charity of others.

Some say if we could afford to buy a bicycle, we would live a flourishing life. When the same people go to a shopping center and see someone with a nice-looking motor vehicle, they become obsessed with the material goods of their neighbors. They are deceived into thinking happiness will be very happy if they obtain a plethora of inanimate objects. Later on, in life when they see a man who owns an airplane, they wish they could have an airplane to travel around the world to make people believe that we are very successful people. Others wish to own a passenger train with our names printed all over and be considered the wealthiest people in the world. Others say, we wish we become a millionaire and buy whatever they want, do whatever they want, and say whatever they want. When millionaires are seated in a room full of multimillionaires, they appear and look like church rats. They are very poor compared to the multimillionaires. In the assembly of rich people, the multimillionaires are considered very poor among the billionaires. Considering the definition of flourishing life given by the Webster's dictionary, who then is flourishing?

As a believer and a fruit bearing Christian, be like a palm tree that gets its success from the soil. The soil is a metaphoric word for our father, the Lord God who is our creator and provider. Although our Lord promises us an abundant life, yet it is a wise counsel to be yourself and learn to accept who you are and who you are not. The highest form of responsibility for a believer is to seek God's favor on your knees. Christians do not crave and fight for material things in this world rather learn to apply the spiritual tool that leads us to living a flourishing life, which is our faith in God, learn to accept who you are and be proud that you are the way you are. You do not have to change the color of your skin, hair, and gender to prove your success in life, or as an indication that you are living a flourishing life.

For decades, I thought I was a mistake in life and opted for a change from any source, which never came and will never come until I meet my Lord to ask him why. In later years, I realized that I can improve on what I have, focus on what I want, and who I was meant to be. Then place focus to be the best I can be in this journey of life. In order to move forward in life, I have to start with accepting who I was and cultivate my mind with repeated transforming words, phrases, sentences, chapters and books from the living word of God about what is important to my survival and those around me. A songwriter's lyrics iterate, "Give as it was given to you in your time of need, and unto your mission be true." This is my philosophy in life, which has led me to living a flourishing life and a blessing to me and my family. To acquire your own concept and inner belief regarding living a flourishing life. Learn to believe in yourself and what you are capable of doing and being. You have all the power you need to achieve whatever you want in life. Sometimes you may experience a bumpy road but that is a part of the fun. Go for it. You are in control of your own happiness so choose to act on it. Cherish each moment

19

of joy as it comes along and prayerfully accept every challenge as a speed bump and not as a stop sign.

A palm tree does flourish in its own way without disruption to the source of support, the soil. When the palm tree explores its seeds, they fall on their own ground and begin to germinate and grow. Palm trees do not uproot another palm to make a way to excel in life. Contrarily, it utilizes its natural ability to deeply extend its roots until it finds the water level and the right amount of nutrients that are needed to grow, multiply and create its own oasis. Unlike humanity, which exploits the resources, time and energy of others to acquire wealth and flourish, palm trees have the ability to create their own wealth and live a flourishing life. As fruit bearing Christian, we must commit to a lifelong journey to achieving a flourishing life. Raise your eyes above your corporate or whatever work, think bigger and smarter. Envision a life lived with purpose and meaning. Then commit to it by learning from people who have gone before or associate with people and learn from them. You will have hardships to endure (Romans 5:3-4). However, God wants us to flourish: "For I know the plans I have for you," declares the Lord, "plans to prosper you and not to harm you, plans to give you hope and a future." (Jeremiah 29:11). These are very grave and serious matters. Do not let your day-to-day life dictate your legacy at work and at home. Find inspirational people, be intentional with your choice and commit to it. There is an interesting story with an uncanny relevance. It discusses a group of professionals that decided to conduct research to find out why some people are very poor, marginal, underserved and living from hand – to - mouth in a society that is filled with opportunities and riches. They also ask why are others so affluent and wealthy in the same society with a doctrine that promises equal opportunities and privileges for all its inhabitants. They used a sample set of twenty people and negotiated with them for their research. Ten of them are very poor and ten very rich. The research group took all the millionaires' dollars from the ten rich people and sent them to the street without a dime. The money taken away from ten rich persons was given to the ten poor people who now became rich. After ten years, the research team went back to see what had happened. Surprisingly, the ten people who got the rich people's money were all on life support in the various hospitals while the rich people who became poor had regained all their riches and were living a prosperous life once again. Therefore, you are always the product of your own thinking. So, stop complaining, access your potential and get to work by depending on God.

Chapter 5

PALM TREES HAVE THE ABILITY TO THRIVE

As a faithful fruit bearing Christian who desires to live the life of righteousness, and be like a palm tree, we do not beg for bread in order to survive. Just as a palm tree works to stretch its roots into the heart of the soil, so are Christians called to work for their living. Having a dime in your wallet or pocket book doesn't mean you are destitute. The reason that Christians do not entertain an impoverished mentality is because our Lord says he will supply our needs according to his riches in glory. Riches where? In glory? Where is glory? Our supply in the glory of God is found in the embodiment of Christians respect for God and worship of his majestic and honoring of the supreme God of all creation. Therefore, we are built to withstand the issue of supply and demand. Our primary objective or delight is to walk by faith. Of course, which most Christians consider this difficult to do. According to the Bible, righteous Christians are built to thrive exactly just as the palm tree is built to thrive under unfavorable conditions. The Lord feeds the birds but he doesn't throw their food into the nest. The depicting characteristics of a righteous and flouring Christians are not their outward appearance, eloquence, and wealth. None of the pertinent influences are embodied on the inside of the individual. Take David for an example. God instructed Prophet Samuel to go to Bethlehem. In the house of Jesse, he was instructed to anoint someone who would replace King Saul of the tribe of Benjamin as king of Israel. When Jesse gladly assembled his children for this awesome occasion, David was left out. According to Jesse, David was considered a child, yet he was out doing the most difficult work that should have been assigned to an adult. The fact that David was out in the field catering to the family business and the adults were home tells more about the role of David in the family structure. After David was anointed as king in the presence of his family, the father demanded that he return back to shepherding the flock. David needed to be trained to take the throne as King of Israel, but he was tied down taking care of the family's business in the field.

So how could he ever do the job for which was anointed? Yet, God has a plan for the shepherd boy who is poised to rise from taking care of animals to taking care of a nation. According to the book of I Samuel 16: 14-23, The Spirit of the Lord had left Saul, and an evil spirit from the Lord was terrifying him. "It's an evil spirit from God that's frightening you," Saul's officials told him, "You're Majesty, let us go and look for someone who is good at playing the harp. He can play for you whenever the evil spirit from God bothers you, and you'll feel better." "All right," Saul answered. "Find me someone who is good at playing the harp and bring him here." "Here is the only resume of David." According to a search team report," they said. "A man named Jesse who lives in Bethlehem has a son who can play the harp," one official said. "He's a brave warrior, he's good-looking, he speaks well, and the Lord is with him." This is the only resume or job description that David had to propel him to the throne. Saul sent a message to Jesse, "Tell your son David to leave your sheep and come here to me." Soon after David was on his way to the white royal palace to become the musical director for King Saul. Terrified, Jesse loaded a donkey with bread and a goatskin full of wine, then he told David to take the donkey and a young goat to Saul. David went to Saul and started working for him in a part-time capacity. David held this part time job just as some of us in America. He played music for king Saul and thereafter his internal evil leaves him and David runs back to the sheep. Saul pretended to like him so much that he put David in charge of carrying his weapons. Not long after this, Saul sent another message to Jesse, "I really like David. Please let him stay with me. Whenever the evil spirit from God bothered Saul, David would play his harp. Saul would relax and feel better, and the evil spirit would go away. Jesse didn't know that there was something inside David that was greater than the whole nation of Israel. David is a typical example of how a palm tree thrives.

Let us discuss Joseph who is also a typical example of a palm tree. He was built with the gift of righteousness and he is surely like a palm tree. Joseph's mother died after she bore Benjamin. Jacob was afraid of Laban who had pursued him when he reported to Jacob that one of the children from his household had stolen his gold. Jacob became furious and out of this fear and pronounced death upon whomever was caught with the stolen gold must die. Shamefully, at the end of the search, Laban's missing gold was found in Rachael's sack. It was Rachael who stole the gold of their father.

Little Joseph was the first of Rachel's sons and Jacob started to grow in wisdom and obedience to the Father's way. He was home with his younger brother conducting a chore for their dad. He was loved according to the Bible.

Joseph began to have dreams and could not keep his little mouth shut about these dreams. He kept telling his dad about them. It was already rumored among his brothers that his dreams were showing who he will turn out to be in the future. Instead of the brothers showing appreciation and blessings on their brother Joseph, he was desperately envied. Joseph didn't know the wicked plan of his brothers but God was in the background working out his plans. One thing about the God we serve is He does not give us updates about His plans for us. Jacob escalated the hatred towards Joseph when he sewed a coat of many colors for Joseph while the other brothers were wearing rags and assigned in the field to take care of the family business.

The ten brothers had been away in the field for a while, so the father asked Joseph to go in search of them and bring back a report. In obedience, Joseph happily left home in haste to find his dear brothers. Venturing afar without an army or bodyguards to protect him, he was angrily seized and his coat of many colors was ripped into pieces. Joseph has gone from wearing a rag to a coat of many colors and then to slave clothes when he was sold to the Ishmaelite traders. The Lord being a master planner, can use whatever means to propel us to living a righteous and flourishing life. While in captivity, Joseph was obviously distanced from reading the scroll on which the word of God had written. He was away from his family, culture, staple, and food yet he stood in obedience to the will and word of God. Joseph was ridiculed, abused, and mocked. Many called him a man who lost his way in life. Yet I can imagine Joseph curled up in the prison cell and crying out to the God of Israel. He couldn't imagine that his own brothers sold him to strangers without remorse and walked away. All Joseph had to do was to anchor his faith in God of the Hebrews and take it one day at a time in Egypt. The wicked design of the brothers towards Joseph did not break him. Instead it propelled him to greatness in Egypt. Yes, indeed the palm tree reminds us that we are created to thrive. As Christians we are not meant to struggle to make it through the week, the day, the next hour or the year for that matter. We are not meant for our world to feel like a debilitating weight upon us. The break of dawn should not be the starter pistol for another meaningless day in the secular rat race. We are not meant to be shackled by anxiety, worry, and fear. No, we are meant for so much more. We are meant to have life and to have it more abundantly. That is the promise of the eternal God for us believers. We are meant to dig deeper, stretching out more to reach out. We are meant to know God and to make him known to the world. We are meant to point to the one hope. The one anchor, and the one true source of joy, peace, and contentment for the entire human race. Mere survival is for those who have no hope. We

23

are not part of those who wander in a limited survival mode. As a child of God, you were created to thrive.

I'm not saying you won't experience trouble in this life. Yes, there are lots of troubles, including disappointments, frustrations, and emotional instability in this world. Only the false teachers and preachers of the prosperity gospel claim otherwise. They promise prosperity when you buy a small bottle of water pitched from a dead sea, a bottle of oil when you kept under your pillar while using Scriptures written from prison, or during some of the lowest moments in the lives of godly men. Without exception all of us will have some bad days. But Jesus tells us to take heart. He has overcome the world, which means we can thrive amidst it all. When I was in college, the word did come alive but it was part of my vocabulary because I knew all along that was the pattern of life. It felt like the best I could do was to survive and not to bring disgrace to my family and myself.

Nominal Christians and carnal minded Christians need to be reminded that the gospel is distinct. Many true, conventional Christians need to hear that, too. The way to respond to a rapidly changing and post-Christian culture isn't to resist change altogether. It's to allow the gospel to dictate what changes are worth making. Many of our churches stand as visible reminders that we've valued our sub-cultures more than the people to whom we have been sent. We often refuse to change on the inside. We would rather follow self-indulgent precepts of other churches, pastors, evangelists, church elders and church outreach ministries rather than flow with the Holy spirit. Culture certainly is always changing, but the word of God will never change. You can resist it or ignore it. If you oppose the word or wish it weren't the truth that won't make it any less real. The more we insist on doing "business as usual" in our churches, the more we'll find ourselves being ineffective and fruitless. If we are going to continue to communicate the message of the gospel meaningfully, our churches must change. In addition to their attitudes towards worship and service.

We don't contextualize to minimize the confrontational claims of Christianity, but to maximize them. It's a matter of putting and spreading the gospel into language or word that our neighbors can hear and understand. In the midst of a society that wants to do away with Christianity, it's easy to fall into the temptation of wanting to make our churches comfortable refuges. But Jesus calls His Church to mission, which means that the way we do church should focus less on our comfort and more on faithfully reaching the lost. If our churches have to be a little more uncomfortable to us insiders in order to reach even one lost soul for Christ, that's a sacrifice we should all be willing to make. Being radically distinct and culturally relevant aren't at odds. They are two sides of the same gospel coin. Jesus came and made his home among us in the most culturally relevant way possible. He embodied the language and culture and traditions of the Jewish people. Some of us have not survived very well. Maybe our circle of friends has changed. Maybe our families are different than they were this time last year. Yet we have managed to survived some major storms. In fact, a lot of us are in survival mode right now. Stop saying things like, " If I can just get married", "if I can just pay my bills", "if I can just take a vacation", "If I can just complete the nursing school", "If I can just get out of an awful marriage", or "If I can just get my children through college" all will be well. You were created with greatness. By faith you call things into existence. If you're not careful, you will live your life with that same survival attitude. How many pastors of fruit-bearing Christians are prepared to spend a week or two in an inner-city shelter or in prison to put it to the test? Can you imagine where Jesus came from to come and live among us? Let us do the same. We are built to thrive.

I left the orphanage mission where I lived and went to school for seven years with hundreds of others from various traditional backgrounds. I went there back to visit several years later to see how my former colleagues are currently filling in the blanks of their lives. Now, as I reviewed 40-year-old photographs taken by the American Missionaries way back when. The pictures are now being kept by Pastor Anthony Sackor. My heart is saddening with grief when I see many are still living a very nominal life just as they were in secondary school. They never grew up although they just grew older. Several others living around the world are doing well and also are filling in life blanks appropriately. We are of the same group, yet they never venture outside of their thinking. They were dying slowly and truly none even reached to live to be 60 years old. We as Christians were not made to simply survive life, work, school, or adverse family issues. You were made to live a flourishing life like the palm tree. You were created for one purpose, to know God and make him known to the world. You are not living the life you were created to live if survival is your purpose.

Chapter 6

PALM TREE CAN NOT BE GRAFTED

Grafting according to Webster's dictionary defines a graft is inserting, transplanting, embedding, attaching, affixing, establishing, joining and splicing of a substance into another. A palm tree has the ability to reject any unwanted or undesirable associations into any part of the structure with any substance that is of a different chemistry and make up. The word of God emphasized the same warning to all believers who are desiring to live in the household of Almighty God. The believers are called to separate themselves from the world because light has nothing to do with darkness. The Bible says, do not be yoked with unbelievers. Very amazingly a palm tree does abide by this principle of God. It's no wonder why the Bible is calling all believers and fruit-bearing Christians to be like the palm tree. When believers form alliances with the world by practicing what the world does it is a straight recipe for backsliding and carnality which has the tendency to make the word of God ineffective, and the church merely serves as a social club. The church of Christ has to be very careful by not incorporating worldly practices in the worship of God. Most Christians and churches are guilty of doing things after the patterns of the world for not allowing the Holy Spirit to direct, inspire, and control the worship service.

A pastor made this statement when he was invited to speak in a church that I was attending. "Today, I am very thankful to God that I am given this awesome opportunity to preach. This is my first time preaching on this topic. I just want to try to preach about this topic and later I will preach it to my church". He sounded like a presidential candidate. No pastor, before preparing a sermon without seeking counsel from the Holy Spirit for a special message he has for his people.

It is said that when you sleep with dogs, you will wake up from bed with fleas. Look around you and see with whom you are confiding your problems. Look across your dining table in the eye of the one sitting across you. Does he or she look like someone who shares your dream, belief, vision, and your values? Can this person foster better values in you? Does this person have the mental, professional, and spirit capacity to help lift you up when you are down or when things you suffered for are slipping away? Can this person be trusted in every way? Does this person fear God? Fearing of God is the beginning of wisdom. Remember when you were in school, there were different types of examinations: There was the true or false. If you close your eyes and circle either one of the two, it is possible that you will make a grade, probably a very good one. There was also the matching type of testing. In this case it is possible that you can easily get a good grade. In addition, there was an essay test. Teachers have become sick and tired of reading the mess created by the flaws in the educational system. They played a significant role in these shortcomings. Therefore, at a minimum your penmanship needs to be excellent. The teacher may even give you a passing grade without reading through the mess you wrote. There was another examination that is called FILL IN THE BLANK. This requires one of two words. This text or examination determines whether you took the time to study or not.

Remember that from the day you were born to the present. You are constantly filling in the blanks of your life. Therefore, when developing a relationship with someone to be part of your spiritual enhancement, ask the question, "how has this person filled in the blanks in their life so far"?

The palm tree is very careful about associations. Associations do matter regarding developing one's character. An old adage says, "show me your friend and I will know who you are." As a Christian, you must prayerfully choose with whom you want to foster relationships. Just as a palm tree you cannot be grafted. Christians must deny all associations and relationships that are repugnant to the Christian faith and denial of Christ. Although a tree is a tree in general, yet a palm tree as a tree will snap when you try to graft it into another tree. A palm tree would rather die than to be grafted with another tree. So, when the Bible says, the righteousness shall flourish like a palm tree, all those who are claiming to be Christians must learn to reassess their connections and relationships. The fabrics, tissues, and entire make-up of a palm is so different and unique in a way that it can never accept to be part of any external make-up. Although many Christians are so weak and complacent, they are unable to set limits and eliminate people who unjustly intrude into their lives and after dumping their dirt, adamantly walk away. Therefore, like the palm tree, righteous Christians are not built to be grafted.

As believers in the death and resurrection of Jesus Christ, we are children of the living of God and saved from condemnation. We are bought with a price. Therefore, we cannot put on the identity of this world. When we receive the gift of salvation our body becomes a living soul and the Lord Jesus Christ, son of the living God, makes us his dwelling place. Our bodies also become the dwelling place or temple of the Holy Spirit. By virtue of our salvation, we are bound to do only what is acceptable and pleasing to the Lord of our lives. We are being transformed from death to life and cannot be part-takers of worldly activities.

Do you remember the story of the three Hebrew boys? Their Hebrew names were Hananiah, Azariah and Michael. The Babylonians did everything to change their identity, belief system, culture and nationalities but they never forget their creator, the God of Abraham, Isaac and Jacob. When Satan got into the head of Nebuchadnezzar, he started his craziness by presenting himself as a god with a golden image. The three Hebrew boys stood up against him while millions of others succumbed to the order of his worship. By order of king Nebuchadnezzar, the musicians sounded the alarm upon hearing every living soul in their reach. When the boys refused to bow to the golden image. The gossipers and backstabbers ran to tell the king that three of the Hebrews boys refused to bow to his god. I like their response when they were threatened to be thrown into a waiting firing furnace. They said, "Oh! King Nebuchadnezzar, we can no longer discuss this matter with you. We will not worship your golden image. Don't waste your time and ours, if you put us into the firing furnace the God whom we serve is able to deliver us. Even if he doesn't, we will not." They were determined to adhere to the commandment that says thou shalt not worship any other god and bow down to them. At the end of the celebrations, the name of the Almighty God was proclaimed. When fruit-bearing Christians take a united stand in the troubled world, things will move in the direction of God's desire for the world. Can today's Christians stand their ground when challenges are unleashed upon the church of Christ? Sadly, Christianity today is compromised in other countries.

Here is another example about Daniel. When Daniel and the three young Hebrews were exiled from Judah into Babylon, they were recruited from among many to be trained in the language and literature of the Babylonian Empire. Instead of politely asking them about their choice of diet, the Babylonians decided to impose their way of life by offering them food that was usually sacrificed to their God and prepared in the context of purity. It was very daring that the boys refused their meal while still In exile and there was no other source of food. They were built like the palm tree. The three friends of which the book of Daniel speaks were Hananiah, Azariah and Michael. They responded," Give us what we need, and we will be good then come after a couple of weeks. So, with all due respect we just cannot eat this food, sorry." Righteous Christians who are like palm trees are very careful about what they put into their bodies. A righteous Christians will not use heroin, marijuana, cocaine, crack cocaine, alcohol and nicotine jeopardizing their precious lives. Your life is no longer yours because a valuable price was paid by Jesus for once and for all no more sacrifice. The desire of craving for drugs or alcohol was paid by the blood of Jesus Christians.

As Christians our makeup is different and although we are still in this world, we must be careful because we are destined for eternity with the Lord wherein the lasting flourishing will take place forever and ever. Here is another reason why Christians must vehemently refuse to be grafted. As Christians we are grafted in Christ Jesus. This doesn't mean we have forfeited our nationality and become Israelite. According to Roman chapter 11, here is how Apostle Paul puts it. The Bible speaks about us being grafted into the same promise given to Israel of Old. For example, Paul in Romans 11 states, "For if the first fruit be holy, the lump is also holy: and if the root be holy, so are the branches. And if some of the branches be broken off, and thou, being a wild olive tree, were gaffed in among them, and with them partakes of the root and fatness of the olive tree; Boast not against the branches. But if thou boast, thou bearest not the root, but the root thee. Thou wilt say then, the branches were broken off, that I might be grafted in. Well; because of unbelief they were broken off, and thou stand by faith. Be not high minded, but fear: For if God spared not the natural branches, take heed lest he also spare not thee. Behold therefore the goodness and severity of Jehovah: on them which fell, severity; but toward thee, goodness: otherwise thou also shalt be cut off." The price of our redemption was paid in full and our salvation is secured. The natural branches of olive symbolize natural-born Israelite and the wild branches represent the gentiles who are grafted in. It's important to realize that the same root, which represents the promise given to Abraham, bears both the natural-born Israelite and gentiles. Paul also warns here not to boast.

Regarding Matthew 3:9, recall when the Jews were responding to John the Baptist and claiming that they were the children of Abraham. From their perspective, this gave them a preeminence as a people. In response, John states that if Yahweh so chose, He could make the rocks cry out. John here is simply confirming that The Lord is not limited by man and that salvation is based on more than ethnicity, as is also seen in Romans 11.

In the third chapter of Galatians, Paul ties together baptism, the acceptance of all nationalities, and the promise to Abraham, "For ye are all the children of God by faith in Messiah. For as many of you as have been baptized into Messiah have put on Messiah. There is neither Jew nor Greek, there is neither bond nor free, there is neither male nor female: for ye are all one in Messiah, The God of Abraham, Isaac and Jacob. And if ye be Messiah's, then are ye Abraham's seed, and heirs according to the promise. One, baptism represents a type of adoption as sons of God." Strictly speaking, we will be sons of God at the resurrection, when we are changed into heavenly beings. There is no separation or distinction in gender or ethnicity. Therefore, the palm tree does not associate with unlike species. Palm trees cannot tolerate unlike species. Don't now allow worldly things into your life. If you allow the world to dictate the life you seem to enjoy in peace today will sink and you cannot ever flourish. Stop entertaining sin if you want to be a successful and flourishing Christian like a palm tree.

In order to grow in life, we need to see that the Christian life is a grafted life (Rom. 11:24; 6:5; Gal. 2:20). Two trees of diverse kinds cannot be grafted. They cannot grow together because they are not of the same kind. Because man was created according to God's kind, man and God can be grafted together. If we are not clear about the principle of grafting, we will not be able to properly apprehend the matter of life. We will make mistakes related to life. Jesus was a fully grafted person, a person of two natures. On the one hand, when He lived on the earth, He was the real God. On the other hand, He was a man expressing God. He was God expressed. So, we also are persons of two natures, the human and the divine. When we receive the divine life, our human life is not ended. Our human life still exists.

Even though the human and divine lives are of one kind, one is stronger than the other. We are now living a weaker life and a stronger life. Whenever a weaker life is put with a stronger life, the stronger one subdues the weaker one. The sisters are the weaker vessels married to the brothers, who are the stronger vessels. For this reason, the wife takes the husband's surname as her own. In this sense, the wives are subdued. On their wedding day, the sisters realize this and put a covering over their head. During the wedding only the husband's head can be seen. This indicates that the two should live one life.

In the meeting we may joyfully proclaim, "I am a part of Christ, I am one with Christ, and I am mingled with Christ." However, after the meeting, we may desire to be the head and want Christ to be the covered one. We must always remember that we are the wife and He is the Husband. As such, we are two persons living one life together without separation. One lives in the other and through the other. This is the way the grafted life can come into being. When we love, we do not love by ourselves. We love with Christ, through Christ, in Christ, and Christ loves through us. This kind of love does not express our human virtue alone, but our human virtue with Christ's divine attributes. His divine love becomes the very essence of our human love. This is not two loves existing together, but one love living in the other. This can be compared to a hand in a glove. The hand and the glove are not two parties merely existing together. Rather, the hand is put into the glove, making the two objects one. When we are loving others, it is Christ who is loving, but not by Himself; Christ is loving through us. He is the "hand" and we are the "glove," not as a pair, but as one in the other. The human life has the divine life within it as its content, and the divine life has the human life as its expression. If this is not clear to us, we can never understand the Christian life.

Chapter 7

LIFE OF A PALM TREE IS ON THE INSIDE

Exactly like the human race, the soul and life of a palm tree lies on the inside and is divinely covered or sealed up with several layers. Is the human body calibrated in layers? Yes, our bodies are shed in layers. Likewise, the structure of the palm tree is divided into layers as well. Let us get it clear that the soul of the human body has the capacity to survive without the body but the human body cannot survive with the soul. The soul is the nature of God and remember when he said. "Let us make man in our own image?" The Lord was referring to the soul and not the color of your skin, our nationality, or creed. In the case of a palm tree, unlike other trees, the core or nucleus of what is the real surviving capacity of the palm tree that is sealed within. The growth, the refreshing, height and width of the palm tree are determined by the inner core of the palm tree from which life originates.

The first layer of a palm tree is referred to as the bark which can be peeled off without causing a substantial hurt to the tree. Although by doing so you are creating a condition that makes it look very ugly and useless. Of the millions of trees in the word, a palm tree is the only unique tree which patterns after humanity because when you peel off the bark of ordinary trees they die. When the bark is peeled off other trees, nutrients needed from the ground through the roots to grow and flourish will be affected. The capacity to absorb nutrients will be restricted and undermined. When the palm tree absorbs the nutrients from the soil, they are transported upward by way of the second layer that lies underneath the bark towards the manufacturing component. If the process is left uninterrupted, the tree remains green then grows and produces fruits and more fruits. As righteous and fruit bearing Christian we must be like the palm tree if we are to flourish in this world and remain green till the church is raptured to be with the Lord forever and ever. Therefore, it is worthy to say that the Lord is very much more interested in how we respond to his will inside of us than what we portray on the outside. The Lord is not interested in how many clothes we wear, the real estate we own, our material worth, how well we sing, how we pray, how we worship, and our personal influences. Instead, he is interested in the life we live for him on the inside.

The Lord looks on the inside not the outward appearance of our bodies. No matter how high, magnificent and large the cathedral, the Lord is not there. He dwells in our hearts. During the ceremony in the home of Jesse in Bethlehem wherein the Lord told prophet Samuel that there is a king among Jesse's children go and anoint him. Very quickly Jesse assembled the children he taught could be the chosen King of Israel. Typical of humanity, prophet Samuel sported a few of Jesse's children and concluded that indeed these men had the posture of a King but the Lord told Samuel to stop looking at these men." I have denied them to be king over my people. Although he looks handsome and puts up an excellent facade, I have weighed him and found him to be a man of less value." This is a testament that the Lord searches our hearts every day to see if we are still standing in commitment to our vow to serve and do his will which is our reasonable service. Secondly, take a look at what prophet Samuel said to Saul when he got sick and tired of searching for his father's missing donkey. Samuel told Saul that the lost donkey you have been looking for is found but spend the night and see me tomorrow because I will tell you what is on your heart. Eureka! Saul has the donkey on his mind and the Lord will tell him what is on his heart. What a mystery? There is a lot that goes on in our minds yet the Lord focuses on what goes in our hearts.

Chapter 8

PALM TREES HAVE
THE ABILITY TO BEND AND NOT BREAK

Just as humanity has the potential to choose and ability to make decisions, to bend or break in the time of upheaval. During predictable or unpredictable circumstances, a palm tree has the affinity to bend in the raging storm and not break. No matter how high, deep or wide a storm may be, a palm tree has the ability to bend and not break. As righteous Christians seeking to be like the flourishing palm tree, beware that there will always be storms or challenges in our lives and in this world. The Lord did not tell us that life will be a bed of roses. On the contrary, he says "I will be with you always". Always means, whether in or under the sea, whether in the winter or summer, and whether your life is threatened and put at gunpoint don't bow or submit to harassment under threat of death, the Lord is standing by you.

As fruit-bearing Christians we are subjected or exposed to challenges like everyone else but the Lord revealed to us through his word He has overcome the world and because He is in us and we are in Him we are also overcomers. So, we are under obligation to rejoice as we celebrate our victorious life on earth. This is the underlying reason Christians are always smiling regardless if life has been difficult. While others who are without Christ are living in misery. Therefore, we are prone to bend and don't break due to our new life after the Lord of God of the universe takes residence in us. Whether it is an indescribable struggle, civil or tribal wars, frustration, depression, unexpected bad news, or a spouse's unceremonious departure from home, we can never break and bow in shame.

There is a spiritual rallying song usually raised by Pastor Morgan in our church. It goes like this:

For as long as the Lord liveth, and seated on the throne we never bow in shame. We can't produce more fruits if we as Christians bow in disgrace or shame just as the world does.

How will you be a witness to someone who needs the Lord when your living conditions are the same? You don't work, you are living on government welfare subsidies, and sleeping in homeless shelters because you don't have the discipline to keep a job, your attitude is indifferent.

The apostle Paul was whipped with 39 lashes on his bare back. He was beaten with rods three times. He was pummeled with stones one time and shipwrecked three times. He was Adrift at sea one night approximately a distance equivalent to a one-day journey frequenting danger from rivers. He encountered danger from robbers, danger from his own people, danger from Gentiles, danger in the city, danger in the wilderness, and danger at sea. He also encountered danger from false brothers during his toil and hardship enduring many sleepless nights, days full of hunger, was often thirsty, cold, and exposed to the pressure of anxiety for all the churches. Just like the palm tree, he bent almost horizontally but never bowed in shame or broke. Are you disappointed in life with your children, spouses, relatives, enemies who seek to destroy you, and promotions that turn into a dismal demotion? These tribulations are intended to break you but because of the Holy Spirit in you, you will never break or bow in shame in Jesus' name. In times past if you fell victim to a worldly existence in several diverse ways and when Jesus took residence in you, the circumstances changed for the better. He is now the Lord of your life and the life you live is no longer yours. So when you find yourself face to face with an apparently insurmountable problem, you can call on him. He knows about what goes on within you so be humble enough to call on him.

Just as the apostle Paul encourages us, "We are hard pressed on every side, but not crushed; perplexed, but not in despair. Persecuted, but not abandoned, struck down, but not destroyed because we will never seize to carry around in our body the death of Jesus, so that the life of Jesus may also be revealed in our body." The presence of the Holy Spirit in our bodies has enabled us to withstand the pressures of this life. Read, listen, or witness the annual onslaught of hurricanes seen most often in the south. Notice there are never casualties that involve palm trees. In every storm or hurricanes, most trees lose their heads, branches and fruits but palm trees remain standing after the storm. It is scientifically proven that palm trees gain more strength when the storm is over and gone. Can fruit-bearing Christians be like the palm tree?

35

Chapter 9

PALM TREES CANNOT BE USED AS WOOD

Like Palm Tree fruit bearing Christians cannot be used for wood. Meaning, those who are called by God in the womb of their mothers and after are destined to live with the Lord in heaven where there will be joy, peace, and happiness. From the day of creation, our bodies are destined for heaven and not in hell where there will be burning and gnashing of teeth. The Bible says, the Lord himself shall wipe away all tears because we have endured the hardship and persecution by ungodly people. Job lamented and stated it desired this way to his colleagues, "I will not bend, give up or bow to what has happened to me. He continues if this matter will result in death then In my flesh shall see God." Job said, "it has been thousands of years ago before the birth of Christ." The apostle Paul says, "we shall see him as he is." Therefore, the palm tree exemplifies an expressed hope of our future. Our souls will be saved and live forever in heaven and will not be subjected to burn because our bodies had the capacity to resist fire.

A story is told about two gentlemen who were born in the same city in the Midwest of the United States of America. Both were neighbors, shared meals together, went to primary and secondary school together. They were drafted by the same football team. At the age 18 both had different aspirations, visions, lifetime plans, and desires. Let us give them names. One is Tom and the other is Ryan. Their parents knew about their childhood relationship so they offered to send them to the same college. Ryan agreed but Tom desires to take another route in life in contrast to his parents' wishes. Ryan completed his undergraduate studies and then went on to study law. After four years of hard work and study, Ryan graduated with a master's degree in law and passed the national examination to become a practicing lawyer. Ryan was appointed to serve as a Federal judge in one of the states in the East Coast. Ryan has married and has three children all of whom are doing very well in school. On the other hand, Tom did not go to college as was the wish of his parents. Instead, he got a factory job right after high school as chief of plant security.

Tom joined a group that was addicted to alcohol and synthetic drugs. Progressively, Tom's lifestyle changed for the worse. He could not maintain any healthy relationship with friends, family, co-workers, and former school mates. Tom's close friends are those who live in the drug infested areas. When Tom became fully addicted, his salary couldn't sustain his addicted habits. He opted to commit criminal acts to support this new lifestyle. After a couple of years of associating with drug users and alcoholics, Tom was arrested for committing a felonious crime. He was charged and sent to court. Ryan, the longtime child friend of Tom, was the judge assigned to the case. The court sheriff escorted Tom into the courthouse and offered him the front row seat assigned to people on death row. Tom was so terrified but when he lifted up his head and saw a man who looked exactly like Ryan, his heart leaped for joy in hope that his verdict would be mitigated. Ryan has noticed also that this guy without doubt is Tom, his longtime childhood buddy. On order of the judge Ryan, the prosecuting lawyer presented his argument that the only punishment that befitted a crime committed by Tom was a death penalty by hanging. After the defense lawyer and prosecuting lawyer spoke, the case was turned over to the jury. After two days of deliberating, the jury came down with a guilty verdict on all counts. The judge motioned to Tom to stand up as he read the verdict. Tom, you are guilty on all counts and must be put to death by midnight. As the police moved forward to curve and get him ready to be put to death, judge Ryan took off his robe and stepped down to where Tom stood as he was being led to the gallows. "Stop", Ryan shouted, "let him loose, he is free to go home. I will take his place so I can release him and let go home to his family. Tom, because of the love I have for you, I will die in your place but go and sin no more." This is what Jesus did for mankind. Christians who are living in obedience, who are disciples and preparing others to be disciples are passed from death unto life. Jesus the son of the living who voluntarily took to scroll, came to earth and was born as a child, grew up among men, experienced no sin, took our sins and nailed all of them with him on the cross. We are free for Jesus has paid the price of sin in full. Jeremiah 31:11 puts it this way, "For the Lord has Redeemed Jacob and ransomed him from the hand of him that was stronger than he. They shall come and shout aloud in the height of Zion and they shall be radiant over the goodness of the Lord." Verse 14 continues, "their life shall be like a watered garden and they shall sorrow no more. It is the same God who planted the seed of everlasting life in our hearts." Our bodies will not be consumed in hell. Remembering the prophet Elijah and how the Bible details how he was escorted upwardly to heaven with a chariot of fire. The bodies of the aforementioned three Hebrew boys were not made or built to be consumed by fire.

In John 4:16 Jesus declares, "I am the way and the truth and the life. No one comes to the Father except through me. "In Acts 4:12 Peter proclaims, "Salvation is found in no one else, for there is no other name under heaven given among mortals by which we must be saved." According to Paul, the faithful will enjoy eternal life, but those who don't know Christ will be punished with everlasting destruction." Thessalonians 1:9 iterates his urgent call, "How can they believe in the one of whom they have not heard? And how can they hear without someone preaching to them?" Romans 10:14 takes such texts at face value. Many evangelical scholars maintain that even those who fail to hear the Gospel through no fault of their own will be damned. Believers or Fruit bearing Christians will not be in hell because they are not built for hell and everything thrown out of heaven will be hell. Therefore, we encourage all believers to adopt the structure of a palm tree which cannot be used as wood for fire.

Chapter 10

PALM TREES HAVE THE ABILITY
TO SHARE EXTERNAL ILLS

A traditional Jewish story was told long ago about a farmer who had many donkeys working for him on his farm. One day as he perused the farmland, he saw a pit which he noticed was hazardous to all workers and villagers who would come to obtain produce either for sale or for consumption. Instead of filling the pit with dirt, he decided to seize the oldest donkey and dump him into the pit alive. He succeeded in catching the donkey and dumped him into the pit. Unfortunately, the body of the donkey didn't fill the pit. So, the farmer invited all his friends and informed them to come and help him to cover the donkey with dirt. They came with shovels, hoes, and diggers. Soon they started throwing dirt over the donkey. As the invitees dumped more and more dirt, the donkey started wailing, shouting and crying for help. Without acknowledging the animal's cries for sympathy, the invitees continued and even intensified their efforts by dumping dirt mixed with rocks and other sharp objects. After an hour of dumping the dirt, the donkey became quiet and inside the pit remained quiet for some time. As the dirt began to pile up more and more, the donkey had figured out a way to shake up the dirt underneath him. The donkey continued to shake up the dirt until he trotted off. If a donkey can learn to escape the dirt, how much can Christians do to release themselves of the burdens that are so easily besetting? Fruit-bearing Christians who are desiring to serve God must learn to apply the same principle as the donkey instead of asking God to take their burden away. Truly, God is well able to take all the burdens away only if you allow him. Scriptures say, it is by the anointing that the yoke will be broken. Meaning, no amount of preaching, singing and dancing in church has the capacity to break the yoke thrown at you by the enemy. Therefore, as a Christian, and more importantly a fruit-bearing Christian strive for God's anointing. According to Hebrew 12:1, we are advised to lay aside those things that make it difficult to serve God fully and to run the race that is set before us. Here is how the writer of Hebrew puts it, "Therefore, seeing we also are compassed about with so great a cloud of witness, let us lay aside every weight and the sin which doth so easily beset us and let us run the race patiently that is set before us."

It is an intriguing thing that we are under obligation to lay aside our weights. Many Bible believing Christians had the notion that it is the Lord's responsibility to take our weights. Those weights were nailed to the cross long ago when Jesus took to the cross willingly. So, there is no other place for God to take our sins and burdens and dump them. Some people are holding fast to their cigarette smoking habits, bottles of vodka, beer, cocaine, heroin, and prescription drugs expecting God to wipe out everything from their backs or hands. We must be like the palm tree if we are to run the race with endurance. The palm tree is built to naturally share its exact baggage and keep producing. It is called self-confidence, self-discipline, spiritually self-assessment, and self-probing. What is some more baggage we carry and expect God to remove and dump somewhere else? Realistically, a Christian cannot serve two masters and effectively be a faithful and a fruit-bearing Christian without a serious spiritual problem.

Palm trees are very different from regular trees when it comes to pruning or sharing excess baggage. Because palm trees are sensitive, it's very important that you take your time when trimming palm trees. Unlike other trees, you cannot cut back the canopy. It will damage the palm tree to the point where it dies. The only time you should prune your palm tree is when the fronds are discolored or broken. This is a form of a natural or self- pruning process. Palm trees get most of their energy from their fronds. So it's important to be careful not to remove too many. The more fronds you remove the harder it will be for them to thrive, and even survive. By trimming your palm tree, it will not only eliminate nesting places for undesirable insects, but also will prevent further damage from happening to your tree. Drug addiction and alcoholism constitute serious baggage. Immoral acts, deception, gossip, malice, and ungodliness are all problems that can hinder spiritual growth. This is what the apostle Paul has to say, "My brothers and sisters who are called unto salvation and proclaimed the Lord Jesus as savior must rejoice." He further emphasizes, "Of course it is not trouble for me to write the same things to you again and it is a safeguard for you."

The apostle Paul says, "For it is we who are circumcised, we who serve God by his spirit, who boast in Christ Jesus and who put on confidence in the flesh. I also have reasons for such confidence. If someone else thinks they have reasons to put confidence in the flesh. I have more circumcised on the eighth day, of the people of Israel, of the tribe of Benjamin, a Hebrew of Hebrews,

40

in regard to the law, a Pharisee gains to me I now consider for the sake of Christ, what is more I consider everything a loss because of the surpassing worth of knowing Christ Jesus my Lord, for whose sake I have lost all things. I consider them garbage, that I may gain Christ and be found in him, not having a righteousness of my own that comes from the law, but that which is through faith in Christ the righteousness that comes from God on the basis of our faith." Paul continues, "that the righteousness that comes from God on the basis of faith. Yes, to know the power of his resurrection and participation in his sufferings, becoming like him in his death, and so somehow, attaining to the resurrection from the dead. Not that I have already obtained all this or have already arrived at my goal but I press on to take hold of it. But one thing I do, forgetting what is behind and straining toward what is ahead, I Press on toward the goal to win the prize for which God has called me heavenward in Christ Jesus."

The Lord had said to Abram, "Go from your country, your people and your father's household to the land I will show you. I will make you into a great nation, and I will bless you and I will make your name great. And you will be a blessing. I will bless those who bless you and whoever curses you I will curse and all peoples on earth will be blessed through you".

Chapter 11

PALM TREES HAVE THE ABILITY TO WITHSTAND SHAME, ABUSE, AND DISGRACE

Unlike humanity, a palm tree has the ability to memorialize abuse, shame, hurts, pain, and disgrace instead of wallowing in deep sadness and vengeance. When you take a look at a palm tree, you will notice several scars from bottom up and a series of rings around the trunk. Those are progress reports of achievements depicting the time transition from difficult and humiliating days to the days of hope and maximum production of more fruits. For believers and fruit-bearing Christians those scars will ultimately become stars when the church raptures. The palm tree has something to show to nature and to the soil which it maintains a permanent relationship with. Bible believing Christians must be ready to give their account when the roll is called at the judgment seat of Christ. In many cases, the bark of the palm tree is often cut off, branches cut off and roots are tempered for no reason of benefits to the palm. In many diverse ways, the palm tree is stripped of its outer layers making it look very ugly, embarrassing, shameful, and undesirable. In spite of this, a palm tree is determined to grow and will never share its feelings to another palm tree, nor complain to the creator. Henceforth, palm trees will begin to rebuild what has been destroyed. The overriding reason is that the palm tree has one major objective, that it must accomplish, and that is to bear fruits and flourish. This is a profound lesson for believers who are being challenged to bear more fruits.

Have you been abused by your spouse? Are you carrying a burden of unforgiving spirit in your heart or your life? Have you been emotionally or physically abused which has caused you pain and sleepless nights? Are you entertaining feelings of being cheated at church, work, and social gatherings? Are you experiencing untreatable health issues, disordered and dysfunctional issues in the family that continue to negatively impact your spiritual growth? Is anyone using you and taking advantage of you without remorse? Remember the profound truth that you cannot eat rat poison and expect the rat to die. If the pain and hurts are kept within, guess who suffers? You will and therefore become unable to be a fruit bearing Christian. Are you feeling downhearted because after working for many years and finding yourself still finding it hard to make it in life? Are you carrying a hidden secret in your life? Are you someone who smiles and laughs with people in the day time but when night comes, you are deeply sad and taking prescribed mental health medication? Are you being treated unfairly and going around with a burden or load of sin? Then this chapter was prayerfully designed and written with you in mind.

Without doubt you are carrying a wound in your heart which will make It very hard to enjoy the spiritual life as a fruit-bearing Christian. An unattended wound in your heart will get infested. An infested wound in your heart as a Christian will give rise to bitterness, sleepless nights, hatred, anger, rage, malice, negative imaginations, wishful thinking, unreliability, dishonesty, and a carnal minded believer. If any of the above listed conditions applies to you as a Christian then, it is no wonder why you are not enjoying the optimal level of blessings as we are destined by God from the time of our birth. It is for this reason that when people sit on the same bench during church service, one comes out rejoicing while the other goes home looking very miserable and depressed. Then when you are asked by a friend who did not go to church, what did your pastor preach about? You have nothing to say because you heard nothing. The body was in church, you took part in the greetings, you sang and danced but your mind was wandering somewhere else when the pastor was preaching.

There must be a release of the curse so the healing of the seriously infected wound in your heart will occur and blessings will begin. You may be wondering why this hasn't happened in your case. In Genesis 22: 1 we are enlightened. Blessings flow from Isaac to all generations. Isaac blessed Jacob which flows from his generation. Esau took on all the curses so don't follow him or emulate his lifestyle. God does pronounce curses and blessings. For example, "I will make thee a great nation God said to Abraham. Truly, a palm tree has the ability to withstand abuse."

What are the various ways that palm trees can be abused? Oftentimes people take sharp objects like cutlass, knives, and axes to cut the bark of the palm tree or the branches without a meaningful purpose. They do this with the intent to hurt the palm tree. The life or core of the palm tree is within and immune to external destruction. Unlike other trees when you cut the bark of a tree the tree will die, the palm tree it only encounters a temporary disheartening feeling.

For almost four and a half decades I have been practicing the act of being like a palm tree. I desired to be unconditionally accepted by colleagues. As a teenager I felt limited and awkward in many areas and stored in my heart deep resentment inadequate towards myself. By the time I reached the age of 20 years old, I was convinced to take my own life because I felt that the world would be a better place without me. There were no medical doctors or miracle working pastors to reverse my predicament. My primary concern was I will never win the love of any woman and no woman who walks on God's earth will ever accept my marriage proposal. Progressively, I managed to have and to keep a covenant friends like my Liberian pastor Anthony Sackor, the late Joseph Nagbe, the late Andrew Naklen, Stephen Kerwillian, Pastor Eric Targbeh, and many others who saw my inner being and did not focus on my outer appearance. The one thing I knew is that I was dearly loved by my parents and saplings, otherwise I would have committed suicide before completing secondary school. I have prayed for years for a life partner, then the Lord heard my cry and led me to a woman who fears and serves the Lord. She has never considered looking at my condition instead she loves me through the eyes of the Lord Jesus Christ. May the Lord bless her soul? I love her dearly. Then I came to the United States of America and ran into a man named Pastor Morgan Ikonne and his family who are now my covenant of friends and pastors. They intern introduced me to a host of friends at the Rebuilders Apostolic Ministries.

Chapter 12

A PALM TREE IS EVERGREEN

Palm trees are evergreen and this revelation speaks to our ability to make sound decisions if we are to remain green and produce more fruits. The human body has three components: soul, body and spirit. Two of those parts need to be fed daily. The body needs food just as the spirit needs food. The one that is fed with more and nutritional meals will grow, flourish and bear more fruits. Just as humanity goes to the shopping centers to purchase food, we must go to other shopping centers to buy food for the spirit. The spiritual meal is the word of God. Imagine if we treat the Bible just how we handle our cellphones. We will grow taller than the palm tree, resilience like the palm tree, evergreen like the palm tree, refuse to associate with individuals who do not share our beliefs, dreams, and visions particularly for God. I vividly remembered a day when I left my cellphone at work. It was like something had departed from my life. I hardly slept all night wondering who had called or had not called. Never has it ever occurred to me that I should treat my Bible the same way. Do I miss my Bible when I go to work? I don't think so. It is a shame for a Christians who have claimed to be stern believers to not treat the Bible more than we do cellphones. Later in recent years I have learned to stay green and flourish. I remembered you must get on your knees and stay in prayer.

Palm trees are forever green in the summer, spring, autumn and winter. Similarly, fruit-bearing Christians who are seeking to live a flourishing life do not wait for a church rival to be on fire for God. To remain green like the palm tree, we must be glued to learning about the Lord Jesus through his word. If we as Christians will read the Bible and pray in the same frequency, we use our phones or attach ourselves to Facebook we should be green in all seasons. For the palm tree to remain green all year round, it must perform the duty assigned to it by the soil and that is taking in the nutrients by way of its fibers and root hairs and utilize them for the sole purpose of production. The palm tree does reciprocate its gratitude by shedding its purged leaves that are further decomposed to fertilize the soil. There are millions of believers who have adopted the culture of calling on God to provide for them. Do these same people have fruit bearing capabilities towards the service of God? No one can please God and remain green without faith. Hebrews 11:6 exemplifies this, "for whoever comes to God must have faith that God exists and rewards those who seek him." A palm tree stretches its roots into the heart of the soil due to unconditional faith it has in the soil. The apostle Paul stresses it this way, "So then, my friends, because of God's great mercy to us I appeal to you. Offer yourselves as a living sacrifice to God, dedicated to his service and pleasing to him. This is the true worship that you should offer." (Romans *12:1) "More* than anything else, however, we want to please him, whether in our home here or there." (*2 Corinthians 5:9) "If* you plant in the field of your natural desires, from it you will gather the harvest of death; if you plant in the field of the Spirit, from the Spirit you will gather the harvest of eternal life. Then you will be able to live as the Lord wants and will always do what pleases him. Your lives will produce all kinds of good deeds, and you will grow in your knowledge of God." (*Galatians 1:10) Instead* we should always speak as God wants us to because he has judged us worthy to be entrusted with the Good News. "Do not try to please people, but to please God, who tests our motives. The world and everything in it that people desire is passing away; but those who do the will of God live forever." (*1 John 2:17)*

Chapter 13

PALM TREES CAN BIND TOGETHER AND PROVIDE A PLACE OF REFUGE

Palm trees naturally grow mainly in the tropical regions of the world including Palestine in the Middle East. Characteristically, they grow together in groups. Seldom, you will find one palm tree growing somewhere. Over a period of time, that palm tree will multiply by producing fruits-bearing seeds that fall to the ground. When the seeds get ripe and fall to the ground they germinate and grow to be another palm tree. Together they form a canopy of shade that serves as a resting place for other living creatures like the reptiles, birds, humans, and others. The community of palm trees usually provides drinking water by means of the oasis. The birds live on the branches, the reptiles find rest and protection between the branches and the palm trunk. The droplets from the living creatures to the ground are used as nourishment for ants and other living things.

The group of palm trees together can also create what we may refer to as a refuge place for the weary souls who are feeling sad, depressed, abandoned, rejected, marginalized, poor, and abused. It is a place where lost souls go to meet with Jesus for the restoration of their shortcomings and/or pitfalls. It is a rest area similar to what we see or have in the United States of America. Drivers use the resting place along the highway to find food, take a nap, or use the bathroom after hours of driving before they continue the journey. It is often referred to as a shelter in the time of storm or inclement weather, protection from danger, and trouble from harm. It is an escape area for relief when placed under extreme pressure. Similar to the place of reflection like the palm tree, the church of Christ was founded by Christ to perform the same role on earth. What Christians refer to as the church is the building that is used as a rallying point or place of Congregational worship. In the same way palm trees are used to serve as a support and feeding for young plants that are struggling to grow and bear fruits. The shade or resting place provided by palm trees are available to anybody any time of the day or night. There are no doors or security to screen those that seek entrance. A group of palm trees promotes and adopts the philosophy of whosoever will may come. The building is the house of prayer and should be left opened day and night. Now since the enemy has devised plans to wage war against the church, the doors are kept locked and pastors have to make announcements as to when doors will be opened to those who want to seek God's favor and blessings in prayer. Furthermore, the church building is used as a basis for support to young and upcoming Christians. Palm trees do share their shades with one another which allows thousands or millions of living beings to find solace. Without doubt, the church of God dwells in the heart of believers of all people who have proclaimed their loyalty to Jesus Christ to be the Lord of their lives.

As a praying believer who is filled with the Holy Spirit and living a life of worship, when you come to the assembly you bring your fire of worship and I bring mine, then together the church comes alive with a total assembly of worship. In this way, people who are weak will be revived, the sick will be healed, doubters will believe, and souls will be saved. This is the universal objective of the church on planet earth. Palm trees do not change or replace their soil. Palm trees remain with the same soil and grow and then break out. Therefore, Christians are not supposed to run from church to church except when they experience God's word is not truly spoken, or where the word of God is thwarted and patterned after worldly practices.

Chapter 14

THE OLDER THE PALM TREE,
THE SWEETER THE FRUIT

Creatures such as reptiles, birds, squirrels, ants, mice, opossum and host of others are constantly on the lookout for fallen ripe palm nuts in any tropical ecology. The fallen fruit seeds are known to be sweet, juicy, and contain a lot of cooking oil. While these creatures are waiting for these nuts to fall, men who also love sweet and juicy ripe palm fruits are also searching under the palm tree every morning for ripe and fallen fruits. The smartest of the creatures who makes the first discovery is the squirrel, then is followed by the birds. The older and sweet fruit bearing palm tree is usually tall and oversees all other trees because it is completely anchored in the heart of the soil. The squirrels and the birds can make their first arrival because they are built to climb to whatever height or crawl around the weight of the palm tree without difficulty. As the squirrels begin their harvest of the ripe and sweet fruit and the birds begin to pick the flakes with their beak, there are pieces of the sweet fruits that drop to the ground and underneath the palm tree. When this happens the race to the feast of devouring the ripe palm fruit begins with stiff competition among various parties. Man can only take notice through and by the long procession of ants and number of birds flying around and landing about the palm tree. How does that relate to fruit bearing Christians and righteousness? In the continuation of our study of palm trees and the spiritual relationship with the community of believers in Jesus Christ, there is no age limitation when it comes to producing more and sweet fruits. The spiritual disposition of fruit-bearing Christians indicates our lights that must shine so that the world will see and follow us to church. The Bible says that we are surrounded by a cloud of witnesses either to accuse us of what we do or did not do. Therefore, as fruit-bearing Christians we grow in grace and in the mighty works of Christ Jesus as they develop more skill and spiritual capability to win others to Christ.

How old was Josiah when he became king of Israel? How old was David when he was anointed to be king of Israel? How old was Joseph when he became prime minister of Egypt? How old was Noah when he built the Ark? How old was father Abraham when he was called out by his ancestors? In the economy of God, there is no age limitation. Daniel and three other teenagers were among those taken into captivity from Judah into Babylon. This is where the same three Hebrew boys from the land of Judah that brought King Nebuchadnezzar to his knees by their refusal to serve another god that was made by man. Therefore, a Christian who doesn't have the ability or capacity to bear fruits and more fruit as required by the Lord cannot teach others to produce fruits. In order words, a Christian must first be a disciple before teaching others to do the same. In addition, there is no retirement in the kingdom of God. No one can say, "I have preached all the sermons in the Bible and I am done." Accordingly, the palm tree is reminding all believers and fruit bearing Christians that there is no age limit to be a pastor, an evangelist, teacher, preacher, Sunday school teacher, usher, cleaning the church, elder, or praise and worship leader. As long as a person acknowledges a sinful nature and decides to give his/her life to Jesus as his personal savior this person can share the experience with others who are greatly distressed. If a Christian is praying and binding the devil, he must be sure that there is nothing binding him as well. Why would a Christian think that some places of work in the church belong to others and not them? I remember at Rebuilder's apostolic ministries, the pastor practically cried for a teacher for the children's church. Each time the pastor asked members in the congregation to volunteer to teach at the children's church the members would simply start looking around to see who other than themselves is best fit for the description of the calling. Jesus is calling all believers to go out and produce many fruits whether rich, poor, young, old, man, woman, white, yellow, black, or brown. Are you 70 years and refusing to join the choir or praise and worship team? Older individuals who have been in churches or going from one church to another do have the experience, knowledge, skills, and wisdom without doubt to become a fruit bearing Christian. I am too. We as adults must set the tone of worship and discipleship or fruit-bearing modalities for the next generation.

What makes the mature produce sweet fruit? It is the long-term experience of being around churches. Listening to various sermons preached, attendance at millions of revivals, and exposure to Bible Studies under the teaching of learned preachers and pastors. In other words, the elder's ones set the example in congregational worship by giving back. They must display obedience by doing the will of God. The older are aware that it is the work of the Holy spirit that sets the agenda of worshiping when brethren come together to give God all the praises. Going back under the shade provided by the group of palm trees, you will find numerous creatures. In the same way, a pastor cannot discriminate when it comes to worshiping with the church body or prospective members. This is the sweeter part of the fruit. Each member comes into the church with more than one burden or besetting baggage. There may be an old burden that has not been laid aside as well as a new one that drives the person to church. So, when a pastor has in his congregation approximately 100 members in the church, the burdens he must prepare himself to address will be about 300 to four hundred. In addition, some members still carry on their back the burden of unforgiving spirits, some marriage separations, abandonment by spouses, homelessness, the vicious cycle of addiction, some post traumatic disorders, chronic mental problems, unbelievers, idolatry, and so forth.

Church is not and has never been a playground and theater. Rather it is a place that believers come to gather to honor God and his son Jesus Christ. Accordingly, there must be a divine calling and acceptance to oversee the church of Jesus Christ whenever and wherever the Lord chooses. When the Lord calls, he anoints, he provides both human and material resources for his work. So as people come into the church, they bring with them the gifts given by the Holy Spirit to be used in the service of God. The effectiveness of the Pastor in charge is determined by the level of fathering and anointing. This is what sets Pastor Morgan Ikonne apart from other pastors. At the Rebuilder's Apostolic Ministries our pastor is called papa and his wife Jennifer is referred to as mama. I love this type of family reference which is given to our pastor and his wife because it shows spiritual intimacy, love, and commitment to doing what he wants to move God's work forward.

The mother palm tree has passed through all the challenges of life. She has been wounded several times by villagers and strangers. Wounded by children who are clueless concerning the significance of this palm tree. There was a palm tree located a block from our hut in the village back in west Africa that was cherished by my dad. Long before my birth, the palm tree had been there and was very loved and cared for by my father. As I grew up, I thought the palm tree was his god but I was mistaken. He placed a mark on that particular palm tree to symbolize ownership. As I began to see life clearly, I realized later that his emotional attachment to this palm tree was because of its fleshly, juicer, and sweet fruit. In life, what you love you cherish. These typical lifetime experiences of pastors and teachers of the gospel are to be shared with the next generation of believers. The pastors, preachers and teachers of God's who have stories to share of a living hope with the hopeless, distressed, and those carrying wounds in the hearts. It is sure that the wounds we carry today will be turned to scars and then to stars when the glorious church on earth will rapture to be with the Lord forever and ever. When your back is finally against the wall and your inner life is inundated with anxiety, fear, sorrow, and ill-health make the decision to bring your burden to the cross of Jesus Christ, there is still room for you. It will eventually lead to further suffering and humiliation when you remain resistant. When you have come to this cross-road, you need a power-pack spirit-filled church and pastor who has worked the mile you are now traveling to lead you right.

Printed in the USA
CPSIA information can be obtained
at www.ICGtesting.com
LVHW051920221223
767140LV00011B/900

9 781960 684196